YOUNG ADVENTURERS
Outdoor Activities in Nature

Written by Susie Rae
Illustrated by Caroline Attia

This book was conceived, edited, and designed
by Little Gestalten

Edited by Robert Klanten, Richard Schmädicke
and Fay Evans

Design and layout by Melanie Ullrich

Typefaces: Tomarik by Mariya V. Pigoulevskaya,
Sketchnote by Mike Rohde, Brother 1816 by
Fernando Díaz und Ignacio Corbo, and Chaloops
by Chank Diesel

Printed by appl druck GmbH, Wemding
Made in Germany

Published by Little Gestalten, Berlin, 2023
ISBN 978-3-96704-744-8

For more information, and to order books, please visit:
www.little.gestalten.com

Bibliographic information published by the
Deutsche Nationalbibliothek

The Deutsche Nationalbibliothek lists this publication in the
Deutsche Nationalbibliografie; detailed bibliographic data
are available online at www.dnb.de

This book was printed on paper
certified according to the standards
of the FSC®

YOUNG ADVENTURERS

Outdoor Activities in Nature

SUSIE RAE
CAROLINE ATTIA

LITTLE
GESTALTEN

CONTENTS

IT'S TIME FOR NEW ADVENTURES!

Today's a great day for budding adventurers like you to get outside and explore. Whether you're a daredevil keen to try a new sport or a nature lover who wants to learn and soak up the sights, there's so much to do when you're out and about! You can try new things, make exciting discoveries, get to know your surroundings, try to spot animals, and even form new friendships. Outdoor exploration is a great way to keep fit and healthy, too.

The best thing about adventures in nature is that you can do them anywhere! You may want to take long trips to places you've never been to before, but you can also start

right at your very own doorstep. You'll be amazed how many interesting things are waiting for you in your local park or even your backyard.

This book is packed with tips, tricks, and fun facts to help kick-start your outdoor adventures, whether you choose to go hiking, cycling, kayaking, skiing, or surfing. You'll find helpful information on camping and animal-spotting, along with advice on how to predict the weather, find your own food, and stay safe.

So invite your friends, get your explorer gear on, and let the adventures begin!

DID YOU KNOW?
Going outside helps create new brain cells. This enhances brainpower and brain activity.

GETTING STARTED

So you want to try exploring the outdoors—but where to start? First things first: you need to decide what you're going to do. Is there an activity you've never done before but have always wanted to try? Well, today's the perfect day to put things into action! The great outdoors might seem daunting at first, but don't worry: start by making a plan, and remember—the most important thing is to have fun.

START SMALL!

Every big adventure starts with the first step, so don't overwhelm yourself until you feel ready.

How to start planning?

Make a wish list! Write down all the things you'd like to try, then pick one of them. Is there something you can do nearby? Ask your friends or family if there's anything they would like to do and then do it together!

Making a Plan

Write down a plan for your adventure before you get going. There are lots of things to think about!

Everybody is different, so make sure you plan an adventure that everyone in your group can participate in. For example, if you have a friend or family member who uses a wheelchair, check in advance if the place you're going to will be accessible to them.

I'm going to try:

I'm going to start at this time:

I'll be back at this time:

I'm going with:

We'll go to:

We'll get there by:

I need to bring:

The weather is forecast to be:

What if something goes wrong?

Don't worry! It's normal for things not to go exactly as planned. Prepare a back-up plan in case something changes unexpectedly.

7

GEAR AND PACKING

Before you set off on an adventure, make sure you have all the gear you need for the activity you have decided on so that you can stay safe while you're having fun. You'll need special equipment for some activities, which you can find out about later on in this book, while you'll only need comfortable clothes for others. And you'll need lots of enthusiasm for all of them!

Spare socks

Waterproof jacket (just in case)

Healthy food for the trip

Water bottle

First aid kit

Sunscreen

Wallet

Camera

Warm layers

Sunglasses

Snacks

Smartphone

Portable phone charger

Thermal mat

Binoculars

Swimsuit

Hat and gloves

Map (or map app)

Pocket tisues

Trash bag

TOP TIPS FOR PACKING

Put the heaviest items at the bottom of your bag.

Collect your food together in a bag to keep it safe from any critters.

Items that you'll use a lot, such as your water bottle, are best packed somewhere you can access easily.

Ask an adult for help setting your backpack straps at the right length. If they're too loose, you might hurt your back.

When it comes to clothes, rolling is better than folding: tightly rolled items take up less space than folded ones.

Don't forget to bring water and snacks for your pets too!

My kit list:

Water
Banana
Magnifying glass
Swimsuit
...

DID YOU KNOW?
Different people need different things. So if a younger sibling is coming with you, remember to pack some of their favorite toys!

CAMPING

There's nothing like spending the night under the stars in the great outdoors. Camping is especially fun to do with friends and can be done almost anywhere, whether that's at a campsite in nature, on a free beach, or in your own backyard. And while it's a great adventure in itself, you can also do it alongside other activities—why not camp overnight during a hiking or cycling trip?

Towel

Camping stove

Camp mugs

Cooking pan or pot

Bug spray

Camping bowls

Thermal mat

Sleeping bag

TOP TIPS FOR PITCHING A TENT

First check the instructions for your type of tent.

Make sure all the poles are sturdy.

Attach all the ropes firmly to the ground using tent pegs, so your tent will be able to withstand stronger winds.

Check that the canvas is pulled taut. If it sags, rain can pool in the roof and your tent might leak.

Camping lantern

Warm clothes

Tent

TYPES OF TENT

Pop-up tent
Setting up: very easy
Sturdiness: low
Weight: heavy
Fits: 1–2 people

A-frame tent
Setting up: easy
Sturdiness: medium
Weight: medium
Fits: 2–3 people

Dome tent
Setting up: medium
Sturdiness: strong
Weight: medium
Fits: 2–3 people

Tunnel tent
Setting up: difficult
Sturdiness: strong
Weight: heavy
Fits: 3–6 people

Bivouac
Setting up: easy
Sturdiness: strong
Weight: light
Fits: 1 person

Food in containers

Making food is one of the best parts of a camping trip. Make sure you have everything you need to store and cook your food.

Never leave food out overnight—you don't want any critters coming to visit! Some places even require you to store food in a locker well away from your tent, because it might attract wildlife. This is especially true in areas where bears live.

CAMPFIRE SAFETY

Check that fires are allowed in your location. Listen to the adults or experienced campers in your group. And always ensure that your fire has been put out before you go to sleep.

SLACKLINING

Do you have a good sense of balance? Then slacklining might be for you! A little like tightrope walking, slacklining involves balancing on a flat, rope-like line tied between two trees or posts. This is a great activity for people new to outdoor activities, as it can be done almost anywhere there are a few trees—a neighborhood park, a forest, or even your backyard.

A balancing aid, like a long stick

A slackline

HOW TO SET UP A SLACKLINE

Find two trees or posts not too far apart.

For beginners, set up your slackline quite low—about knee height.

Tie your slackline to the two posts. Make sure it is secured tightly. If you're using a proper slackline, ensure the ratchet is locked or you could fall.

For your first few times, have an adult double-check the tension and the ratchet.

KEEPING YOUR BALANCE

If you start to lean too far in one direction, try shifting your weight onto your other foot to keep from falling.

Keep moving! You're much less likely to fall if you're walking than if you're standing still—just like when you're riding a bike.

Holding a long stick spreads your weight out over a larger area and makes you less likely to fall.

Everybody falls sometimes! When you do, try to roll over your shoulder or hip, as this will spread out the force of the fall and help you land more lightly. The more often you fall, the less scary it will seem!

Once you're good at balancing, try some tricks like swinging, jumping, or changing direction. Or what about juggling while balanced on the line?!

GEOCACHING

Geocaching is like a huge, outdoor treasure hunt. You can do it almost anywhere, as long as there's a geocache hidden somewhere. You'll be surprised by how many caches are hidden all over the place. You can even try making your own!

A smartphone with a geocaching app downloaded

What exactly is geocaching?

It's an activity where people use a special app to hide containers, called geocaches, at different locations around the world and then challenge others to find them!

The geocaching app uses GPS to guide you to hidden caches. This will get you within about 10 meters (30 feet) of the cache—the rest is up to you and your geo-senses!

What is a geocache?

Geocaches are usually small, waterproof containers. Inside, there should be a logbook that you can add your name to. They may also contain little trinkets.

14

The best thing about geocaching is that you can do it alongside other activities, such as hiking, cycling, or even while you're walking to the shops.

Never leave anything valuable inside a geocache.

Geocaches are sometimes disguised as something else, so keep your eyes peeled!

WHAT TO WRITE IN A LOG

Thank the creator of the geocache for leaving it. A lot of work goes into creating a cache and it's nice to be appreciated!

Write about how you found the cache. Were you on a short walk or a big hike? Did it take you long to find? Who were you with?

Leave a drawing you did during your adventure.

Talk about how much fun you had finding the geocache! What were the best parts of looking for it?

Make Your Own Geocache

Find a container.

Make a logbook and enter a first log.

Think of trinkets to include.

Hide it somewhere for other geocachers to find.

Make it available to others who use your geocaching app.

HIKING

One great thing about hiking is that you can do it almost anywhere. You don't need a vast forest to traverse or a mountain to climb, you can go for a hike around the countryside, on the beach, or even in a city. It's a perfect way to get outdoors, explore new places, and take in the landscape. It's also great for spotting birds and animals.

DID YOU KNOW?

You don't need to buy brand new equipment—see what you have at home first. If you don't have hiking boots, sturdy sneakers or winter boots will do.

Lightweight jacket

Knapsack

Water bottle

Camera

Long pants

Sturdy boots

WATCH OUT!

Reaching the summit of a mountain and taking in the view is an experience like no other! If you're going mountain hiking, make sure to stick to the paths and be very careful where you're treading—it might be slippery or uneven.

Hiking with a grandparent is the best!

Your grandparents may not be as quick as you are, but they will know the best places to visit and the most interesting routes to take. And they will probably bring some delicious picnic food along with them!

Foraging is great to do on a hike at any time of year! There might be berries and mushrooms in the area you're exploring. Make sure you check with an adult before eating anything you find—you shouldn't put something in your mouth unless you're completely sure it's safe! If you're not sure, take a photo or draw a picture and leave the plant where it is.

Take home memories of your trip! An excellent way to do this is to bring a notebook with you, so you can take notes or make drawings of interesting plants and animals you see on your hike.

Scavenger Hunt

How many of these items can you find on your next hike (or on this page):

Red flower

Bird of prey

Interesting stone formation

Bird in a tree

Berries or fruit

Lookout point

River

Animal on the ground

Fish in the water

Cloud shaped like an animal

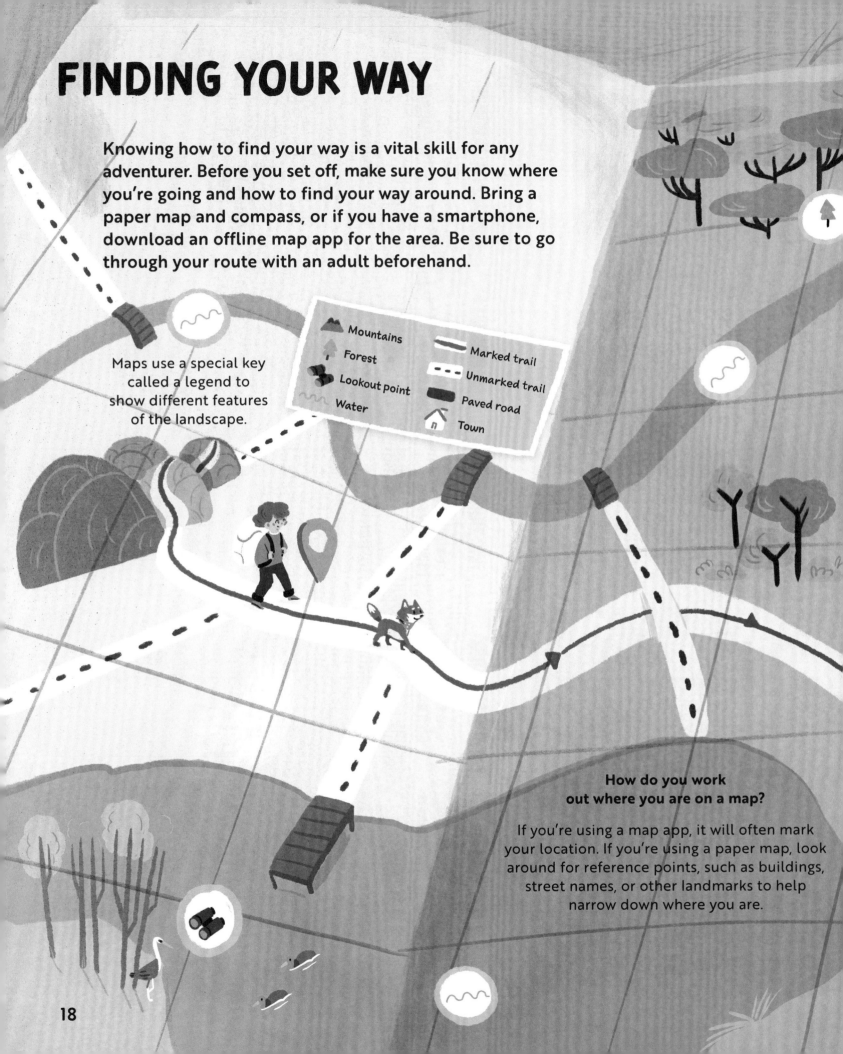

FINDING YOUR WAY

Knowing how to find your way is a vital skill for any adventurer. Before you set off, make sure you know where you're going and how to find your way around. Bring a paper map and compass, or if you have a smartphone, download an offline map app for the area. Be sure to go through your route with an adult beforehand.

Maps use a special key called a legend to show different features of the landscape.

Mountains

Forest

Lookout point

Water

Marked trail

Unmarked trail

Paved road

Town

How do you work out where you are on a map?

If you're using a map app, it will often mark your location. If you're using a paper map, look around for reference points, such as buildings, street names, or other landmarks to help narrow down where you are.

USING A COMPASS

What is a compass?

It's a handy tool that explorers have been using for thousands of years to help them find their way. The needle on a compass always points north.

How does it work?

A compass needle contains a magnet, which is drawn to the huge natural magnet under the North Pole.

How do you use it?

Use your compass with a map. Place the compass on your map and make sure the needle lines up with north on the map. This will help you work out which direction you're facing.

DID YOU KNOW?

Some birds navigate using the Earth's magnetic field, as though they're living compasses!

Try making your own map!

Draw out the area you want to map. This might be your local area, your backyard, or your bedroom.

Come up with a legend like the one on the opposite page.

Mark a specific location with an X. Then give it to a friend or family member and challenge them to find their way to X.

CLIMBING AND BOULDERING

Are you a brave explorer? Sure you are! So if you want to try something a little more adventurous, give climbing and bouldering a go! These exciting and gravity-defying activities involve clambering up and over rocks or climbing walls, using ropes or crash pads. They are a fantastic way to build self-confidence, train creative thinking, and get fit. And nothing is more rewarding than the feeling of reaching the top!

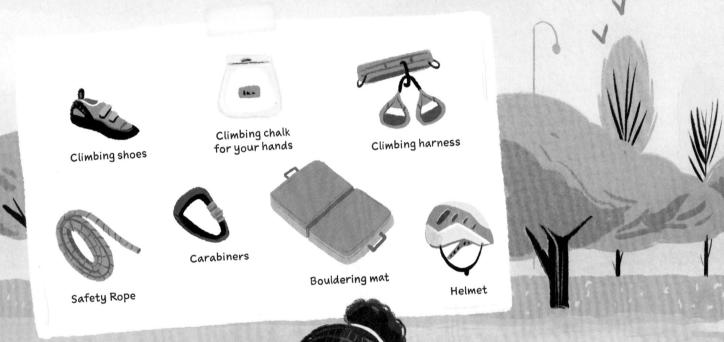

Climbing shoes

Climbing chalk for your hands

Climbing harness

Safety Rope

Carabiners

Bouldering mat

Helmet

You can climb and boulder up cliffs, mountains, and rock faces. See if there are any indoor or outdoor climbing walls near you that you can visit if you want to try something a little less...rocky.

What's the difference between bouldering and climbing?

Climbing involves a harness and a rope, while bouldering is a simple form of climbing over smaller areas near to the ground with no ropes at all. To protect you from falls, you use a crash pad instead.

TOP TIPS FOR CLIMBING

Use your feet. Your legs don't tire as quickly as your arms, so try to put weight on your feet as much as possible.

Take breaks. Climbing is hard work and uses your whole body, so be sure to take time to rest—and drink plenty of water.

Be kind to yourself. Climbing can be difficult at first and it takes strength and skill. Just keep it fun to begin with and you will get better before you know it!

Use "quiet feet." Try to place your feet as silently as possible. This helps you pay attention to your footwork and helps prevent slips.

Don't look down! The prospect of falling can be scary, but just stay focused on the tasks ahead—looking for the next handhold and moving on up.

Don't be scared of falling! You're safe as long as you climb with a rope or use a pad while bouldering. If practiced beforehand, falling can even be fun!

ALL FOR ONE, ONE FOR ALL

Exploring the outdoors is for everybody, so it's important to have the right attitude. If we're smart, careful, supportive of each other, and respectful of the environment, then we'll all be able to enjoy the great outdoors whenever we want— and what could be better than that?

DOS AND DON'TS IN NATURE

Do stay on the trail. Other areas may be dangerous, or you might risk trampling on an animal's habitat.

Don't touch baby animals. The mother might come along to protect her babies, or the smell of a human might cause the animal's family to reject them. So look, don't touch!

Do take or draw pictures. Nature is beautiful but should always be left where it is. Pictures can help you remember your adventures.

Don't feed animals. They are in their native ecosystems, so they know how to hunt and forage for their own food, and human food can be very bad for them. This includes ducks and swans at the park.

Do take all your stuff home with you— including trash! Don't leave anything behind.

HOW LONG DOES TRASH TAKE TO DECOMPOSE?

PAPER
one month

APPLE CORE
two weeks

PLASTIC BOTTLE
500 years

BANANA SKIN
six weeks

GLASS BOTTLE
1–2 million years

DISPOSABLE CUP
50 years

SODA CAN
200 years

CHIP PACKET
80 years

Leave only footprints,
take only pictures.

DOS AND DON'TS IN GROUPS

Everybody is different, so it's important to make sure you're all having fun.

Don't lose your temper. If you disagree with somebody else while you're on an adventure, calmly explain your point of view and make sure you listen to theirs.

Do share your food and water supplies with your group—well-fed adventurers are happy adventurers.

Don't leave anybody behind. An adventure can be ruined by somebody getting lost or feeling left out.

Do take plenty of breaks. If you push yourself too hard, you might get hurt or too tired to complete the adventure.

What Would You Do?

1. **You're on a hike in the woods and your younger brother is feeling tired and wants to stop. What now?**

a) Tease him.
b) Go on without him.
c) Get the group to stop for a break.

2. **It's lunchtime on your trip. What do you choose to eat?**

a) Chips and a brownie.
b) Nothing.
c) A sandwich and a banana.

3. **You disagree with a friend about which path to take. What now?**

a) Cry and shout at them.
b) Split up and take your own paths.
c) Discuss which would be the better path, then all keep going together.

Answers: if you picked mostly cs, well done—you have an excellent outdoors attitude!

CYCLING

It's time to get on your bike! Whether you want to explore a mountain trail, go on a quiet countryside trip, or explore a town or city, cycling is the best way to get around quickly and it can be done almost anywhere. You can do this alone or with family and friends, and can even include it as part of a bigger adventure—why not cycle during a camping trip, or ride your bike on your way to a swimming or slacklining location?

The right kind of bike for your adventures can make all the difference! Casual bikes are perfect for city roamers, road bikes suit going fast and far, and mountain bikes are the right choice for rougher terrain.

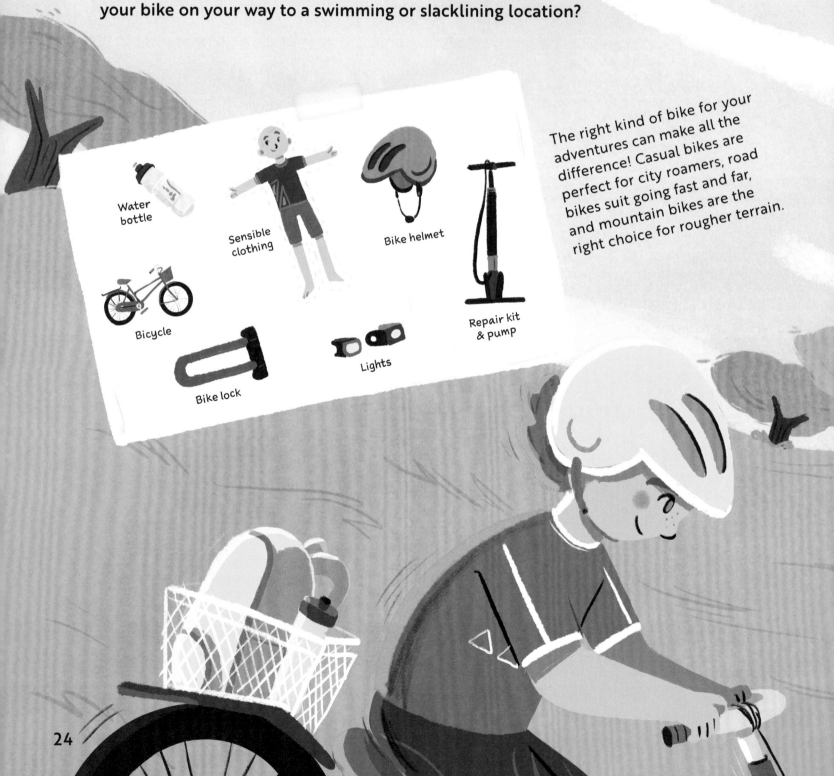

Water bottle

Sensible clothing

Bike helmet

Bicycle

Bike lock

Lights

Repair kit & pump

It's important to stay safe when you're out and about on your bike. Wear a helmet and bright clothing so that vehicles and other cyclists can see you easily. Helmets will protect your head if you have an accident, so make sure you're wearing yours properly.

Put the helmet level on the top of your head.

Close the buckle under your chin.

Your saddle height is right if you can reach the ground with your toes.

THE ANATOMY OF A BIKE

Rack

Saddle

Handlebars

Frame

Gears

Pedals

Chain

Back wheel

Brake

Front wheel

How do bikes stay up?

The spinning wheels create something called a "gyroscopic effect," where a moving object wants to keep moving in the same direction. This means that your bike will stay upright as long as it keeps moving but will fall over when it stops.

SWIMMING

Who doesn't love splashing around in the water? Swimming is a great way to keep fit and have fun, whether you're at your local swimming pool or wild swimming in a pond, lake, or by the shore. Also, you don't need loads of complicated gear to do it, so as long as you have a swimsuit and a safe body of water, you're good to go!

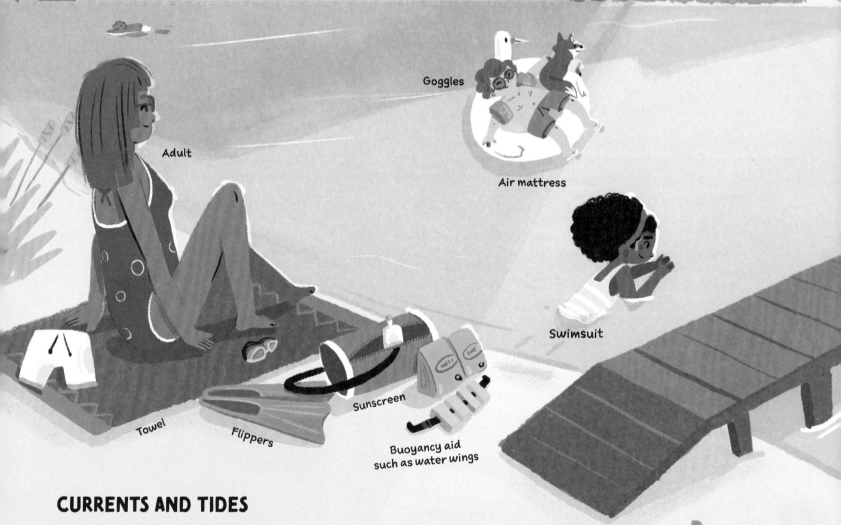

Goggles

Adult

Air mattress

Swimsuit

Towel

Flippers

Sunscreen

Buoyancy aid
such as water wings

CURRENTS AND TIDES

Even if the water seems very calm, rivers and the ocean are constantly moving. There are currents that you don't always see and they can be very strong! They can drag you away from the shore or even under the water. Adults or lifeguards will be able to tell you where it is safe to swim.

Tides are the rise and fall of sea levels—that is, when the water is closer or further away from the beach. Did you know that they are caused by the sun and the moon? Their gravitational pulls cause the Earth's oceans to bulge out at the sides, causing two high tides and two low tides every 24 hours.

THERE ARE FOUR DIFFERENT TYPES OF SWIMMING STROKE:

Breaststroke. Push your arms forward underwater, then pull them to the side, then in toward your chest, and repeat. At the same time, kick your legs out and then pull them in like a frog.

Backstroke. Reach forward with one arm over your head, then pull it back underwater, then do the same with your other arm. Use one arm after the other. At the same time kick your legs in a fluttering movement.

Front crawl. Reach forward with one arm over your head, then pull it back underwater, then do the same with your other arm. At the same time kick your legs in a fluttering movement.

Butterfly. Keep your feet together and kick them like a dolphin's tail. Your arms should make the same motion as front crawl, but you use both at the same time.

SWIMMING SAFETY TIPS

Never go swimming alone.

Wear a swimming aid.

Stay close to the shore.

Stay in sight of your parents and friends.

Never go out of hearing distance.

In thunderstorms stay out of the water.

Beware of waves and strong currents.

Wear swimming shoes. Rocks can hurt your feet!

KAYAKING AND CANOEING

If you're a water lover, you must try kayaking, canoeing, or paddleboarding! It's brilliant to do with friends and opens up a whole new world that's waiting to be discovered in and around the water. Ducks and their curious ducklings might come to say hello, schools of fish might zip past, or you could be lucky enough to spot fascinating forests of underwater plants. Even better, every break is a perfect opportunity to go for a swim.

Dry pack
(to keep your
belongings dry)

Life jacket

Swimsuit or clothes
you don't mind
getting wet

Paddles

Kayak or canoe

Getting into any type of watercraft can be tricky as they rock in the water and might make you fall in before you've even got started! Here's how to get into one without getting wet.

1. Place your kayak or canoe in shallow water, near the shore or dock.

2. If you can, ask a friend to help steady it.

3. Hold firmly onto both sides of the boat to keep it steady.

4. Place your feet right in the middle and slowly lower yourself in.

5. Make sure your paddle is close by so you can grab it as soon as you're seated.

If you're paddling about in a place where it gets choppy because of wind or motorboats, try to meet the waves face on. The bow of your watercraft will cut through the waves and let you ride them out. If a wave hits you side-on, you might capsize (flip upside down in the water).

Professional kayaks are designed to roll if you capsize, meaning you can easily flip yourself back upright. This is a fun and useful skill to learn at a kayak school.

SAFETY

Always listen to the most experienced person.

Stay away from large boats and ships.

Stay close to the shore—don't head out into open water.

Stay together in a group.

Look out for each other—nobody should be left behind!

Life jacket

Wetsuit for cold water

Paddleboard

Paddle sports are a great way to discover amazing underwater worlds. What can you see around or beneath you? Do you recognize any birds, animals, or fish? Make a wish list of the animals you would like to see on your next visit to the water!

Can you spot any of these watercraft next time you're outdoors?

Rowing boat

Paddleboard

Raft

Kayak

Pedal boat

Canoe

SURFING AND SAILING

Did you know that people have been surfing and sailing for hundreds of years? Before boats with engines were invented, people would use boats powered by the wind to travel across the seas. And surfing was invented as far back as the 12th century by Polynesians, whose culture meant they spent lots of time in the water. Today we mostly do these activities for fun and enjoy the effortless movement!

Swimsiut or wetsuit

Life jacket

Rope

Surfboard (or sailboat)

Dry pack

CAN YOU SAIL AGAINST THE WIND?

You actually can! Sailing boats can change the orientation of their sail(s) so that the force of the wind is turned into forward movement. And if the wind is directly ahead, they can just zigzag to move forward.

You need knowledge and skill to go sailing and surfing, so it's a good idea to look for sailing and surf schools to teach you the basics. They will often let you rent a boat or surfboard so you don't have to buy your own.

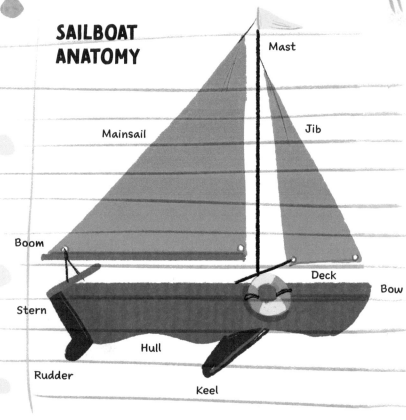

SAILBOAT ANATOMY

Mast

Jib

Mainsail

Boom

Deck

Bow

Stern

Hull

Rudder

Keel

HOW DOES SURFING WORK?

There are two forces involved in surfing: buoyancy (which helps you float) and gravity (which makes you fall down). When you surf, the two forces work against each other—gravity is pulling you down, while buoyancy is keeping you up, allowing you to stay upright and ride the waves.

Windsurfing is a combination of surfing and sailing, using a special board with a sail.

Wakeboarding involves standing on a board and being pulled behind a motorboat.

Wave surfing is when you stand on a board and ride waves as they roll toward the shore.

Sailing can be done in one-person, two-person, or larger boats that are propelled by a sail or multiple sails.

Kitesurfing also uses the wind: a big, sail-like kite is attached to the surfer.

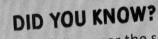

DID YOU KNOW?

If you don't live near the sea or a lake, you might still be able to give surfing a try. In some places there are wave pools where artificial waves are created to surf on. Or why not try surfskating, where you "surf" the sidewalk by your house (if it's safe to do so)?

WEATHER WATCHING

The weather can be unpredictable and change quickly, which can affect your outdoor plans. Always check the weather forecast before you set off, so you can plan for the day properly. It can also be helpful to learn how to read signs of changing weather, so you don't get caught by surprise!

Keep an eye on the wind, as it is often the first sign of a change in weather. If it starts to get windy, it may be shortly followed by rain.

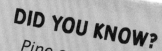

Weather apps are a great way of keeping an eye on the weather. You can even set alerts so that you know if a big weather change is on its way.

Low-flying birds can be a sign of rain. When it's about to rain, the air pressure drops and insects no longer get carried high up into the air. As many birds feed on insects, they fly lower too. There's an old saying that goes, "Hawks flying high means a clear sky. When they fly low, prepare for a blow."

Different climates pose different challenges. Northern areas are often colder, while deserts are often very hot, with very little water. Know the local climate so you can plan properly.

BE ALL EARS!

"The calm before the storm" is more than just a saying. Often birds and insects stop singing or making sounds when bad weather is coming. This spooky silence tells you that the weather is about to change.

CLOUDS ARE OFTEN A SIGN THAT RAIN IS ON THE WAY—BUT NOT ALWAYS!

Gathering wispy cirrus clouds
The weather is about to take a turn for the worse.

Fluffy cumulus clouds
Good weather.

Thick, gray altostratus clouds
Overcast skies and drizzle.

Towering cumulonimbus clouds
A storm is coming.

Low, dark gray nimbostratus clouds
Rain or snow.

OUTDOORS MASTERCLASS

Now that you've found out a little information about some of the things you can try in the great outdoors, it's time to take the next step. These tips and tricks will help you become an expert explorer...and will help you make smart decisions when you're out and about on your next adventure.

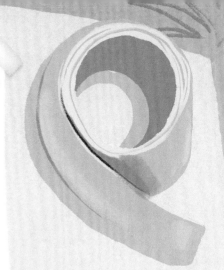

If a member of your group gets bitten or stung by an insect, remove the insect as quickly as possible. Then clean the bite with antiseptic wipes, and if it itches, rub some bite cream on it.

How do I go to the bathroom in the wild?

Find somewhere away from a water supply and dig a little hole in the ground. Cover it up when you've finished and take any toilet paper or other trash home with you.

When sleeping outside, wear lots of layers to keep warm. You lose a lot of heat through your hands, feet, and head, so gloves, socks, and a hat will help you stay cozy through the night.

How to Make a Water Purifier

Cut a plastic bottle in half. Flip the top half over and put it in the bottom half to make a funnel.

Place a filter in the funnel—use a coffee filter or something fabric, like a clean sock.

Now add your filter material. This could be pebbles, sand, or cotton balls.

Pour the water through the filter and watch the clean water trickle into the bottom half of the bottle.

Remember: only use clear, running water, as murky water from still bodies of water, such as ponds, can be dangerous.

Listen to the locals. Local people know their area better than anybody and will be able to give valuable advice. They will know if a path is open or closed, when the weather is likely to turn bad, or where to find the next bus stop.

Carry some duct tape or fabric tape on your adventures. Things can break in the wild, but it's amazing how many things can be repaired with a piece of strong tape!

35

PLANT IDENTIFICATION

It's impossible to step outside without finding dozens of different types of plant. Whether you're in your backyard or local park, up a mountain, exploring the countryside, or even walking down a city street, plant life is everywhere! There's so much to learn from the trees, flowers, and foliage all around us, so grab a guidebook or app and get spotting!

Guidebook and camera

There are thousands and thousands of different trees, but they mostly fit into two groups: coniferous and deciduous.

Coniferous

Sometimes called "evergreen."

Green all year round.

Leaves shaped like needles.

Often produce cones.

Deciduous

Bloom in summer.

Change colour with the seasons.

Lose their leaves in winter.

Often produce fruit or flowers.

Some countries like trees so much they have a national tree.

Canada: maple tree
India: banyan tree
Greece: olive tree
Yemen: dragon blood tree
Germany: oak tree
Senegal: baobab
Maldives: coconut palm

DID YOU KNOW?

Trees can live for a really long time and each year they grow a little bigger. Scientists believe the oldest tree in the world is a Great Basin bristlecone pine known as Methuselah in California. Methuselah is about 5,000 years old!

Some herbs growing in nature can actually be used for cooking to make our food taste delicious. These include fat hen, sorrel, chickweed, wild garlic, and even beautiful dandelions. Make sure to use a guidebook or ask an experienced adult before eating any plant!

Smartphone with identification app downloaded

Much like animals, many plants have defense mechanisms to keep them safe from predators. Be very careful when touching plants, as some might sting or cause a rash. Don't eat anything unless an experienced adult tells you it's OK and make sure you wash your hands regularly.

WINTER ADVENTURES

Outdoor fun isn't just for the summer—there are so many fun activities to try in the winter, especially if you're in an area that gets a lot of snow. All you need is a hill, some friends, and a thirst for adventure—there's nothing more exciting than zipping down a snowy slope at what feels like a million miles an hour!

Ski poles

Snow goggles

Warm clothing

Ski boots

Skis

Snowboard

Sled

Sledding is the easiest of all winter sports. This is just sliding down any snowy hill on a sled. If you don't have one of your own, improvise! You could use a tray or plastic laundry basket.

Skiing involves strapping two skis to your feet and travelling across the snow. You can go fast down a hill or use cross-country skis to trek across a wintry landscape.

Snowboarding is a little like skateboarding, but on snow. Grab your board and go!

Ice skating can be done at ice rinks, or on frozen lakes or ponds if it's safe to do so. All you need is a pair of ice skates.

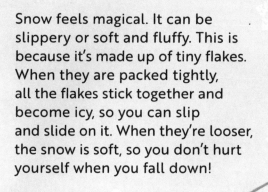

Snow feels magical. It can be slippery or soft and fluffy. This is because it's made up of tiny flakes. When they are packed tightly, all the flakes stick together and become icy, so you can slip and slide on it. When they're looser, the snow is soft, so you don't hurt yourself when you fall down!

DID YOU KNOW?

You can ski in the desert too! Some people in hot areas do sand skiing, shooting down sand dunes. In 2010, Henrik May set the world record for sand skiing, reaching a speedy 57.24 mph (92.2 km/h).

STOP HERE!

The first thing you should learn before you start zooming down hills is how to stop properly—because you don't have brakes like on a bicycle!

When you're skiing or snowboarding, always stay with your group and stick to marked routes. Snow is a lot of fun, but it can be dangerous, so don't go wandering off and take unnecessary risks.

If you love winter activities, there's a whole separate Olympic Games for it! The Winter Olympics happens every four years, with the best athletes in the world competing in sports including skiing, ice skating, and luge (high-speed sledding).

Is my snowboard the right fit?

When picking a board, stand it upright and compare its height to yours. If the end of the board reaches between your chin and nose, it's the right size.

HORSE RIDING

Calling all animal lovers! Horse riding is an extra-special outdoor activity because it not only allows you to experience nature from a different angle, it also comes with a brand new friend! Horses love to get out and about just as much as you do and can help you to explore parts of the great outdoors that you might not be able to reach on foot.

Stables

Bridle

Helmet

Food and water

Reins

English style saddle

HAPPY HORSES

Once you learn to understand the sounds and body language of a horse, you will always know how it feels. Just like you, it feels best when it is well fed, healthy, and fit. And after a day out, horses love to get rinsed off with water, because they sweat too. When they're clean and refreshed, make sure you give them a good stroke—they love it and they'll be so happy to see you the next time!

Horses are friendly animals, but they can be unpredictable. Move slowly when you're near the horse so that you don't startle it. Talk to it in a gentle voice so it knows where you are and that everything is OK.

Mane

Saddle

Reins

Tail

Nose
(for stroking)

Stirrup

Forelegs

Hind legs

Hooves

Horseshoe

Remember that horses are living beasts. Treat your horse as you would treat your best friend.

Pommel

Western-style saddel

The two main types of horse-riding style: English and western.

In **English** style, saddles are light and small. Reins are held in both hands and riders wear a helmet as well as jacket, jodhpurs, and jodhpur boots. You will often see English-style riding at dressage events, show jumping, or sports like polo.

Western-style saddles are larger, with a very pronounced pommel. The reins are held in one hand, leaving the other hand free. Riders are typically dressed in comfortable clothes like jeans, shirt, boots, and a hat. Riding western style is perfect for when you're on long trails or rounding up cattle.

DO YOU NEED A "DRIVER'S LICENSE" FOR A HORSE?

If you're confident and experienced, you can ride your horse on a quiet road. Some places might expect you to have a license if your horse has a carriage or cart attached, but not for the horse itself.

ANIMAL WATCHING

We share our incredible planet with millions of different birds, animals, and bugs, so let's get to know them better! Bird and animal watching can be done anywhere in the world, even from your bedroom window! The creatures you find will be completely different depending on where you are in the world, so why not start a log to keep track of the critters you spot in different places?

Binoculars

Notebook

Pen or pencil

Camera

Smartphone

Guidebook (or app)

To become an expert nature detective, you will want to learn how to look out for traces of different creatures in nature. Keep your eyes peeled for things like footprints, birds' nests, scratch marks on trees...and even animal poo!

Can you spot any of these footprints next time you're outdoors?

Cat

Boar

Duck

The birds and animals you see might change as the seasons do. Animals like hedgehogs and bears hibernate during the winter, while some types of birds will migrate south to warmer climates. Many species breed in the spring, so keep an eye out for ducklings and lambs during that season! Some creatures even change how they look in the winter, such as the stoat or short-tailed weasel.

DID YOU KNOW?
Stink bugs get their name from the gross smell they emit to ward off predators.

Identifying bird and animal sounds is a great skill for any budding wildlife explorer to learn. You could use an app to help you work out what to listen for. What creatures can you hear around your home?

Always remember to be safe and respectful when animal spotting. They may be fascinating but you are a visitor in their home. Keep your distance and never approach or disturb any creatures that you spot.

SAFETY FIRST

Having fun is important when you're exploring the outdoors, but it's even more important to make sure you stay safe while you're on your adventures. Learning your limits and looking after yourself when you're doing outdoor activities will keep you from getting sick or hurt—meaning you can have fun for longer!

FIRST AID KIT ESSENTIALS

Adhesive bandage and dressings

Bite and sting cream

Burn dressing

Hand sanitizer

Gloves

Scissors

Eye drops

Gauze

Antiseptic wipes

BASIC SAFETY TIPS

Always tell your parents where you're going and when you plan to be back.

Bring a first aid kit with you.

Do your research before you set off—what's the area like?
What will the weather be like?
Is there anything to be aware of?

Listen to the adults and more experienced members of your group.

Take things slowly. Rushing can lead to injuries, so take your time and enjoy yourself.

Dress for the weather and the activity.

Be aware of the local wildlife.
Even dogs and swans can be dangerous if you approach them.

STAYING SAFE IN A THUNDERSTORM

Get low to the ground. The safest place to be is indoors or in a car.

Get out of water if you're in it or doing an activity on it—electricity and water are a bad mix, so make for dry land quickly.

Don't shelter underneath a tree. If it's struck by lightning, you might get hit by falling branches.

If there's nowhere to shelter, lie down flat on the ground.

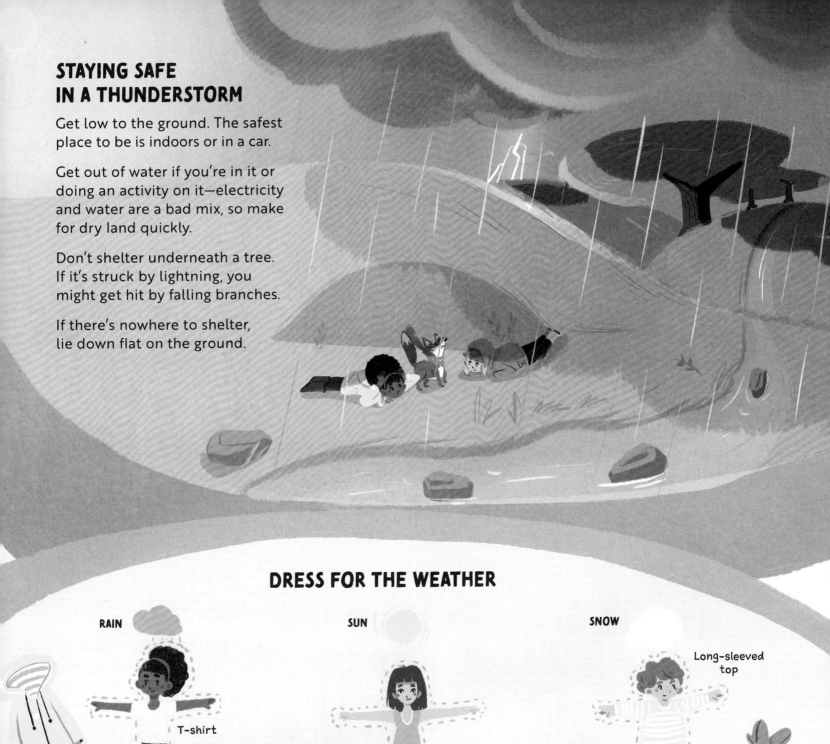

DRESS FOR THE WEATHER

RAIN

T-shirt

Long pants

Waterproof jacket

Umbrella

Rain boots

SUN

Sunhat

Shorts

T-shirt

SNOW

Long-sleeved top

Long pants

Gloves

Warm jacket

Warm hat

Choosing the right clothing for the weather can make all the difference! You'll be able to have fun for longer and won't get tired as quickly. Choose water-repellent gear on rainy days, lightweight clothes on hot days, and properly warm clothes in winter so you won't freeze.

THE OUTDOORS, THEN AND NOW

People have lived with nature for hundreds of thousands of years. From the Stone Age to the present day, human beings have had a strong urge to explore the great outdoors. Before houses were invented, living outside was a fact of life. But in more recent centuries, as life and work became more remote from nature, using the outdoors for leisure activities has become more common.

Kayaks were invented by native tribes in the Arctic more than 4,000 years ago. They would use these to safely travel through the icy Arctic waters. Today, kayaks are used around the world for sport and leisure, but people native to these cold areas also still use them for transport.

For thousands of years riding horses was a necessity as there was simply no other quick means of transport. Today, people in industrialized countries no longer depend on horses to get to places or transport goods. In these places, horse riding has mostly become a leisure activity.

Going for a hike today is one of the most popular outdoor activities around the world, but that hasn't always been the case. In the 18th and 19th centuries, the beautiful landscapes painted by European artists were a major influence in getting people to spend more time in nature.

The invention of bicycles improved life for many people. Suddenly, it was possible to get around a lot more quickly! People soon realized that cycling could also be fun. The Englishman Thomas Stevens was so excited, he became the first person to cycle around the world…on a penny-farthing!

People living nomadic lifestyles have lived in tents for thousands of years. The traditional yurts of Mongolian nomads are still used today and can house whole families! For the type of weekend-camping trips we take today, we use much lighter and smaller tents, whose origins date back to the 1920s.

Sailing ships were once the only way to transport heavy goods across the seas or explore new lands. In modern times, sailing is no longer necessary, as we have powerful engines to propel ships around the world more reliably. Yet the spirit of adventure lives on and drives many people to enjoy sailing cruises as a leisure activity.

GLOSSARY

Air pressure: the weight of the air in the atmosphere resting on Earth. Air pressure changes with weather.

Anatomy: the structure of a living organism or an object explained in detail.

Antiseptic: a liquid used to clean wounds to prevent infections.

Bivouac: a temporary shelter in nature, set up for no more than one night at the same place.

Bridle: a piece of equipment used to direct a horse. Bridles are usually made up of leather strings.

Buoyancy: an upward force that water exerts on an object so that it floats.

Climate: the average weather conditions at a place over a period of time.

Climbing chalk: a white powder used by climbers to keep their hands dry and increase friction for safer climbing.

Current: a powerful flow of water within a river or the ocean that can be difficult to spot and sometimes even dangerous.

Decomposition: the natural process of things breaking down into tiny pieces or getting transformed into different substances.

Ecosystem: a community of all organisms living in a particular area in nature.

Foraging: looking for food in nature.

GPS (or Global Positioning System): a network of satellites that helps us find out exactly where we are on Earth.

Gauze: A very flexible material used for bandages in first aid kits.

Gravity: a force that exists between larger objects and pulls one closer to the other.

Gyroscopic effect: how a rotating object like a bicycle wheel keeps stabilizing the quicker it spins.

Habitat: a place in nature where animals and plants naturally live.

Hibernation: a deep and prolonged sleep that some animals fall into during winters in colder climates.

Highlining: a special form of slacklining very high above the ground for the extremely experienced. Highliners are secured to the slackline with a rope so they cannot fall.

Legend: a box on a map that explains a set of symbols used on the map. These map keys make it easier to read a map.

Magnetic field: a field with magnetic forces surrounding Earth and magnets.

Migration: animals moving from one habitat to another once or twice a year.

Native: a person, animal, or plant that lives in the same area they grew up in.

Nomads: a community of people with no permanent home, who traditionally travel from place to place.

Surfskating: skating with a special type of skateboard with flexible front wheels that offers a ride experience similar to surfing.

Tide: the rise and fall of sea levels caused by the gravitational pull of the moon.

Water purifier: a tool used to filter water to make it safe to drink.